Math Monsters

CALCULATING AREA

Space Rocket!

Based on the Math Monsters™ public television series, developed in cooperation with the National Council of Teachers of Mathematics (NCTM).

by John Burstein

Reading consultant: Susan Nations, M.Ed., author/literacy coach/consultant

Math curriculum consultants: Marti Wolfe, M.Ed., teacher/presenter; Kristi Hardi-Gilson, B.A., teacher/presenter

WEEKLY WR READER®
EARLY LEARNING LIBRARY

Please visit our web site at: **www.earlyliteracy.cc**
**For a free color catalog describing Weekly Reader® Early Learning Library's list
of high-quality books, call 1-877-445-5824 (USA) or 1-800-387-3178 (Canada).
Weekly Reader® Early Learning Library's fax: (414) 336-0164.**

Library of Congress Cataloging-in-Publication Data

Burstein, John.
    Calculating area: space rocket! / by John Burstein.
      p. cm. — (Math monsters)
    Summary: The four math monsters show how to calculate area as they help Mina
figure out how many tiles they need to make their new rocket launch pad safe.
    ISBN 0-8368-3804-1 (lib. bdg.)
    ISBN 0-8368-3819-X (softcover)
    1. Area measurement—Juvenile literature. 2. Geometry—Juvenile literature.
[1. Area measurement.] I. Title.
QA465.B897   2003
516—dc21
                                                2003045010

This edition first published in 2004 by
Weekly Reader® Early Learning Library
330 West Olive Street, Suite 100
Milwaukee, WI 53212 USA

Text and artwork copyright © 2004 by Slim Goodbody Corp. (www.slimgoodbody.com).
This edition copyright © 2004 by Weekly Reader® Early Learning Library.

Original Math Monsters™ animation: Destiny Images
Art direction, cover design, and page layout: Tammy Gruenewald
Editor: JoAnn Early Macken

Printed in the United States of America

1 2 3 4 5 6 7 8 9 07 06 05 04 03

You can enrich children's mathematical experiences by working with
them as they tackle the Corner Questions in this book. Create
a special notebook for recording their mathematical ideas.

Area and Math

Through the use of pictures, children are able to represent
mathematical ideas in a concrete way. This is especially
helpful in exploring the concept of area.

Meet the Math Monsters™

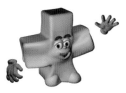

ADDISON

Addison thinks
math is fun.
"I solve problems
one by one."

Mina flies
from here to there.
"I look for answers
everywhere."

MINA

MULTIPLEX

Multiplex
sure loves to laugh.
"Both my heads
have fun with math."

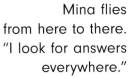

Split is friendly
as can be.
"If you need help,
then count on me."

SPLIT

We're glad you want to take a look
at the story in our book.

We know that as you read, you'll see
just how helpful math can be.

Let's get started. Jump right in!
Turn the page, and let's begin!

One day, Mina flew home to the Math Monsters'
castle. No one else was there. She sang,
    "Where is everyone? Are you playing hide-and-seek?
    Will you be back very soon or later on this week?
    I feel a little sad when I am all alone.
    Is anybody here, or am I on my own?"

Multiplex shouted, "We are outside. We are getting ready to blast off into space."

Mina flew outside. She asked, "Can I go? What will we ride in?"

"Look behind you," said Multiplex.

What do you think Mina will see?

Mina saw a brand-new rocket ship!
"Wow!" she said. "Where did that come from?"
"It was a gift from our cousin, Ivan Idea," said
Addison.

Mina looked down at the grass next to the rocket. She asked, "What are those lines for?"

"Those lines mark the area of our launch pad," said Addison.

"Lunch pad?" asked Multiplex. "Did someone say lunch? Is it time to eat?"

"No, Multiplex," said Split. "We said launch, not lunch. The launch pad is where the rocket stands before it blasts off."

What shape is this launch pad?

"The launch pad is a square," said Split. "All the sides are the same length."

"The rocket gets very hot when it blasts off," said Addison. "It will burn the grass."

"That is not safe," said Mina. "Let's cover all the area of the launch pad with fireproof tiles."

"How many tiles do we need?" asked Mina.

What can the monsters do to find out?

"Let's draw a picture of the launch pad and fill it in with tiles," said Mina. "We can count the tiles to find out how many we need."

"Pictures are fun to make," said Multiplex. "Can we each draw one?"

"Sure," said the other monsters.

When the monsters were done
drawing, Multiplex held up his
picture. He said, "Look at mine."

"That is very pretty," said Mina,
"but I do not think it will make a
safe launch pad."

"Why not?" asked Multiplex.

*What do you
think is wrong
with the picture
of the launch pad
Multiplex drew?*

"Your tiles are all over the place," said Mina.
"You have left lots of spaces. The tiles do not cover
all of the area. Some of the grass may burn."

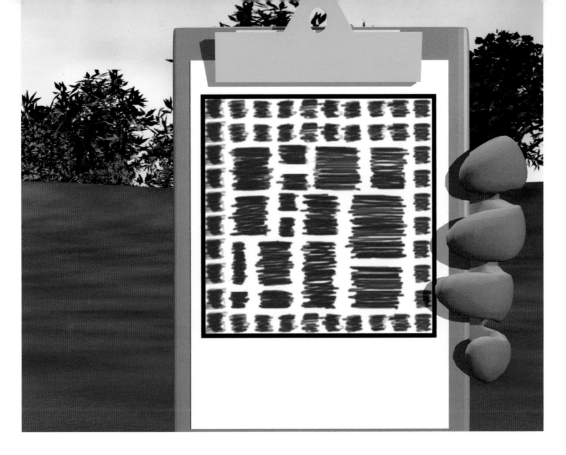

Addison held up his picture. "My tiles are a lot closer to each other, and they are in rows," he said.

Do Addison's tiles cover all of the area?

"There are still lots of spaces in your drawing,"
said Split. "We need to cover all of the area in the
square. The tiles need to be lined up side by side
in even rows."

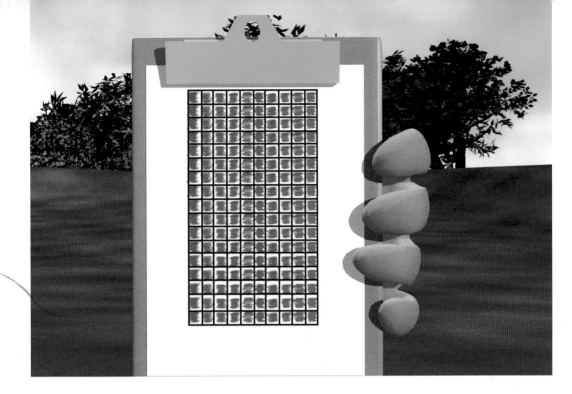

Split held up her picture. "All my tiles are the same size," she said. "They are lined up side by side in even rows. You can see that they cover all of the area."

"That is very nice," said Mina, "but there is something wrong with the shape of your picture."

Do you see anything wrong with Split's picture?

"Your picture is a rectangle. It has two long sides and two short sides. It is not a square like the launch pad," said Multiplex.

"Remember, in a square, all the sides must be the same," said Addison.

"Oh, I see," said Split. "I drew too many rows."

Mina held up her drawing. "My picture is a square," she said. "It is ten tiles long and ten tiles wide."

"I think that is the best drawing of all," said Addison.

Why does Addison think Mina's drawing is the best?

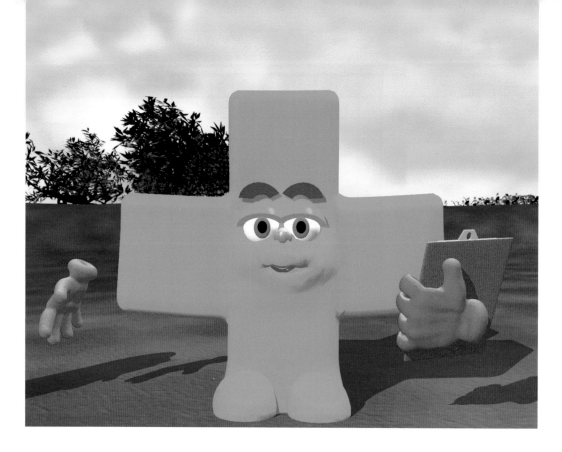

"All of your tiles are side by side in even rows," said Addison. "They cover all of the area. They cover every space — no more and no less."

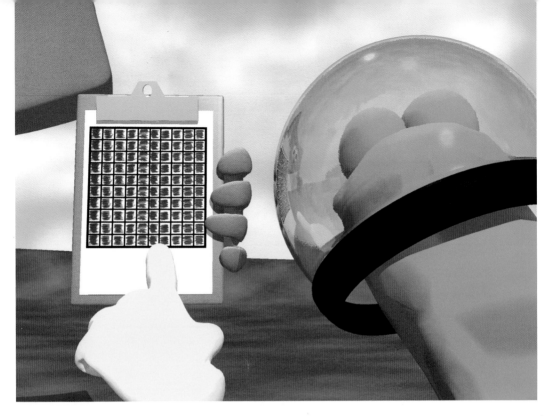

"Annie Ant has lots of fireproof tiles in her shop," said Multiplex. "Let's count the tiles in Mina's picture. Then we can tell Annie how many we need."

"Remember, it is ten tiles long and ten tiles wide," said Mina. "We can count by tens."

How many tiles will the monsters tell Annie they need?

The monsters counted by tens. "10, 20, 30, 40, 50, 60, 70, 80, 90, 100!"

Multiplex called Annie Ant. He said, "We need one hundred fireproof tiles, please."

"I will send them over today,"
said Annie. "To be sure I send all
you need, I will number them from
one to one hundred."

*What will the
monsters do when
the tiles come?*

1	2	3	4	5	6	7	8	9	10
11	12	13	14	15	16	17	18	19	20
21	22	23	24	25	26	27	28	29	30
31	32	33	34	35	36	37	38	39	40
41	42	43	44	45	46	47	48	49	50
51	52	53	54	55	56	57	58	59	60
61	62	63	64	65	66	67	68	69	70
71	72	73	74	75	76	77	78	79	80
81	82	83	84	85	86	87	88	89	90
91	92	93	94	95	96	97	98	99	100

When the tiles came, the monsters covered all of the area in their launch pad.

"It is just right," said Mina. "We have ten rows with ten tiles in each row."

"Now it will be safe when the rocket blasts off," said Addison.

The monsters put the rocket on the launch pad.
"Can I go first?" asked Multiplex.

"Sure," said Addison. "When you
come back, we will each take a turn."

The rocket was ready. The monsters sang,
"Get set to blast off with a roar.
10, 9, 8, 7, 6, 5, 4.
Our countdown song is almost done.
Just three more numbers: 3, 2, 1.
Blasting off is so much fun!"

*Where have you
seen tiles used
to cover an area?*

ACTIVITIES

Page 5 Ask children what clue the picture gives them about what the monsters are up to.

Page 7 The monsters are using a square launch pad. Ask children to find other square areas at home or in school.

Page 9 Provide drawing materials so that children have the opportunity to model the problem-solving strategy of the monsters. Discuss how pictures can be used as problem-solving tools.

Pages 11, 13, 15 A challenge for young children when exploring the concept of area is understanding that leaving gaps or stretching beyond borders can lead to inaccuracies. Use the monsters' pictures to highlight problems in covering area.

Page 17 Help each child draw a large square on graph paper. Ask children to count the smaller squares inside their large ones. Compare their squares to Mina's. How are they the same? How are they different?

Page 19 Have fun with different counting strategies. Children can count by ones, twos, fives, or tens to find out the number of tiles in Mina's picture.

Page 21 Using graph paper, outline an area ten squares by ten squares. Number the squares in order from 1 to 100, but leave several squares blank. Work with children to fill in the missing numbers.

Page 23 Identify rectangular and square areas around you, such as walls, floors, ceilings, and doors. Help children notice the ways these surfaces are covered. You can enrich this activity with a trip to a flooring or tile shop.